SOUL AWARENESS:

A Guide's Message

Katharine Mackey

For Gary, who insisted.

CONTENTS

PREFACE

I first channeled Gerod in the summer of 1987. My meeting with him was not by chance. Throughout my life, I'd been interested in metaphysical concepts and included them in my pursuit to understand life. My husband shared my interest, and together we pursued spiritual matters through our reading, personal conversations, and contact with other people.

In 1987, I was working part-time for a group of psychologists. In casual lunchtime conversations, it became apparent that one of these psychologists also had an interest in metaphysical principles. He and I had a discussion about the book *Far Journeys*, by Robert Monroe, in which Monroe discusses his out-of-body experimentation and the encounters that he and others had with sentient beings. This conversation led to a discussion of communication with spirits through the use of the Ouija board, automatic writing, mediums, and channels.

As a youngster, through the occult interests of family members, I had been exposed to the concepts of ghosts, poltergeists, and communicating with the dead, and I had even successfully experimented with the Ouija board and automatic writing. However, at that time I was ill prepared to understand what was occurring and, turned off by the gamelike quality of these communications, abandoned any further practice of them.

But in 1987, with God centered in my life and with greater understanding of the metaphysical universe, it felt natural to revisit automatic writing. On a warm summer afternoon after putting our young children down for naps, I set about to recreate the experience. Sitting in a chair with a notebook and pen, I felt calm and peaceful. I said a prayer, and in less than a minute, my hand and the pen began to move across the paper.

Gerod's first words to me were: "You are not alone. You are with me. My name is Gerod."

For the next hour, I sat and became acquainted with Gerod. I was never frightened, for I understood and felt within me the presence of the Light, the touch of God that reassured me that all was well. Gerod told me that he is my personal guide, that he has been with me all my life, and that he will always respond to my call. And he has; I never doubt his presence in my life. Over time my ability evolved, and I made the step from automatic writing to verbally channeling Gerod.

Gerod states that he is here to offer assistance to us in our quest to understand who and what we are. He teaches that we each have within us the ability to be our own teacher, our own guide. He says we each have the capability to connect to high-level guidance through our intuition, and he is here to help us understand and to do that. While Gerod and I have worked with many people, a most significant body of work has come out of our relationship with Thomas Zinser, EdD, the clinical psychologist who shared my metaphysical interests. It is through Tom's work with Gerod and with his clients that he has developed a process for emotional healing called Soul-Centered Healing.

I have participated in Soul-Centered Healing and also know many individuals who have benefited from this work. I cannot begin to put into words the awe I have at its power to change lives. What has also come out of Tom and Gerod's work together is a body of information that changes the way we see and experience our world. Through channeling Gerod, I have been honored to participate in the assembling of information that can greatly affect lives and, thus, the world.

The information presented here is not a random compilation but was written directly by Gerod to be shared.

INTRODUCTION

I am a guide from the Light, and God is the source of that Light. The information I share may be new to your conscious mind, but at your soul level this knowledge already exists. The proof of this is your reaction to the information I share. The words of truth resonate; the energy of it goes deep within to your soul, the source of truth within you.

If you remain open to considering the information I share, if you undertake this journey of exploration, you are opening to the knowledge that spirits do exist, and you allow yourself to determine my validity as well as yours. The readiness to begin this spiritual odyssey is signified by your willingness to listen and discern from the heart. For those who feel they are not yet ready for this journey, I wish you well.

There are many areas open to our exploration, and as we explore, I hope to answer many questions for you. However, while some answers will be to your satisfaction, some will not be, as truth can bring up some questions for which only you have the answer.

We shall begin.

1

☀

GOD IS ALL

God is. You are. Because you are, God is, and because God is, you are. There is no separation. God created you and loves you freely, completely, and unconditionally. God created you to love you and to express through you in your experiences in physical form.

I will attempt to describe to you from my point of view what God is. I will tell you God is beyond description, because description, in any language, is limiting and exclusive, and God is absolutely without limit. God is all. All that exists in your physical reality is part of God, from people to animals, to flowers, to waters, to hills and trees, from the tallest of buildings to the sleekest of airplanes, to the sweetest of singing voices, and to the most magnificent art. All things, living and nonliving, all things existing that you can see, touch, hear, or smell are of God; they are energy created into form. From where does that energy come? It comes from God. God created energy; God is energy.

This is my basic understanding of God. In this understanding comes the realization of what energy can become when it is imbued with thought, which is awareness and the ability to create out of that awareness. God is a profound energy that I cannot fully describe but that I can feel. Each soul is encapsulated energy that originated from that energy I call God. Each soul mirrors God, its Creator, through its ability to be aware and to create its own reality. Awareness gives birth to thought, which is a most powerful force. Through thought we perceive, and thus create our existence.

Because all souls came from that same source of energy, which is God, they are the same, and they are one with God. Yet they are different, because the expansion of a soul into a state of awareness is a unique journey.

Many ask me, do I know God, have I seen him, am I close to him, can I define him? If I could describe to you the greatest love and joy you could ever feel, and magnify it to infinity, I could then tell you what God is.

It takes many words to describe God—words unspoken, words hushed, and words spoken in awe. Words held with great reverence within the deepest and purest part of your being. I know God, as do you: through the heart, that part of our being that reaches out and feels the radiating warmth of God's absolute empowering love.

My joy is being close to God. You are close to God also, only it is difficult to realize that, as your view is obscured by your physical body. I am here to help you know God in the physical as well as you know Him when you are in the spirit realm between lives. You have not "forgotten" God. You have only been challenged with the task of seeing God from a different point of view.

In order to create us, God expanded like the cell that multiplies and divides itself into many parts. We are a part of God, and the parts of a whole create the whole, so as parts of the whole we all are God. As a part of the whole, we have the responsibility to emulate the whole. Therefore, we strive to be what we perceive God to be: a being of love, peace, and compassion.

Do not be afraid to acknowledge your oneness with God. To do so is to welcome God into your life and into this world.

God loves you. You are a being created in love, by love, for love.

2

SPIRIT GUIDES

I would like to introduce myself; my name is Gerod. I am a being, an entity without physical form. I am a soul without a body and am referred to most commonly as a spirit, or as those who come in order to assist are called, a spirit guide. In choosing to communicate with you in this way, I am facilitated by a physical partner who serves as the viaduct to connect me, one who is without form, to your world of form. She allows me to use her body and language to communicate with you. Commonly, she is known as a person who channels and that is a term of acceptability to her and to me. She has consented to allow me this access, and it is with her cooperation and permission that this work is done.

Spirit guides are God's promise to you that you will never be alone as you journey into and through the world of matter where you seem to become distanced from God. In religious history, many references are made to angels. We are in essence these angels. We are here to help you feel your connection to God.

God created all souls at one time. When physical life habitation for souls began, there were certain souls who elected to be the guides for those who were leaving the spirit realm for a physical reality. These guides remained in the spirit world to be a connecting link in the spirit realm for the soul in body. The guides are their anchors, the connection to where they came from and to what they know.

In that beginning time, I chose to be a guide, and as such I have guided and assisted within both the physical world and the spirit world. This is work I love and am privileged to do. Many people ask if I have ever lived on Earth in a physical body. I have never physically incarnated through the birth process. I am well aware it is a wonderful experience, but my choice to remain a guide is rewarding and enjoyable. As a guide, I have the privilege of experience and relationship with those souls who choose to live in physical form. Souls in the physical body are beautiful expressions of God, and I am awed by your courage and tenacity.

There are other questions I have been asked which may interest you. For example, can I take shape? Yes, I most certainly can, and I have. I have created

3

for myself a human form through which I have visited your physical world for a brief period. I have flown as a bird, drifted as a cloud, nodded in the wind as a beautiful May flower. I have floated on the autumn stream as an oak leaf and drifted on the snowy winds as a particle of ice. All I have created for myself, you, too, in spirit form, will create for yourself.

People ask if I have guided others. Yes; I have been around since the beginning and have guided many souls. Dependent upon the time and place, and the work needing to be done, I encounter the soul who will be my physical partner and the connection is made. Not in all of these situations, however, have I made myself as consciously known as I do now.

I am also asked if I am my partner's personal spirit guide or merely one who is allowed access through her. I am her personal spirit guide. I have been with her in this particular Earth incarnation from the moment of her conception. She and I have not only a friendship, but also a working relationship born out of contact made before this life. When in negotiation for this life experience, she agreed to assist in the work of spirit by becoming a channel for me, and others like me, in order to aid our assistance to the people of Earth. I also assist her in learning more about herself and her relationship to the Light. Because of the nature of our relationship, I also work through her to assist others.

People ask if I work with others in the way I work with her. No, I channel through no one else. However, I assist others and will work with others, at the soul level. For those whom I have met and worked with, I am available. If they call my name, I hear and I direct my energy to them. Just as you now read these words and have awareness of me, you may call out my name and I will hear you and direct to you my response of energy.

Do I enjoy meeting and talking with people? Yes. You are my friends and I seek to assist you to an awareness of who you are and what you are.

3

CREATION

God's greatest gift to each soul is free will. To ensure the integrity of that gift we must have the freedom to choose; free will does not become a gift of love and validity unless there are choices to be made. Therefore, God did this: with the assistance of the universal energy of all souls, he created this physical reality you know as Earth.

Earth is a world of matter, governed by the laws of nature and the laws of the universe. Souls who participate in a life cycle in human form on Earth are governed by these laws and the restrictions they create. To exist in a world of matter, to relate to the environment and to participate within it required each soul to don a body of matter. A soul in a body is housed within energy denser than itself. This causes a lack of communion, at least initially, between the soul and the intelligence of its physical body. Thus, another restriction imposed upon the soul in the physical reality.

It would appear that the soul in the physical body is quite limited in ability. You need to understand, however, this is not truly a limited state of existence. The soul, being the high level infinite that it is, has the ability to penetrate all restrictive barriers to bring understanding and high level energy into this physical reality, by establishing communication with the human body it is within and that, in essence, it is.

Many people view the soul's existence in the physical reality as an experience to be endured; one that will hopefully earn one the right to leave the physical reality of Earth forever. However, Earth is not a prison, but a school. Its purpose far transcends the belief of it being a harsh and bitter test, a place to strive to leave. God's blessing of love and free will means that we have absolute choice. We experience physical incarnation in order to experience choice.

Life experience is about emotion—reacting, creating, and recreating. Through the process of experience and choices, you begin to understand unlimitedness. How can a soul truly understand how unlimited it is until it first understands what it is to be limited? How can you know what God is, what the light is, until you feel yourself in a body in the physical world sensing separation from your source, which is God? How can you know the aspects of God's love, until you experience the emotional aspects of being God's love? God gives you a great gift in the ability to choose and this is experienced and learned more fully in a world of spontaneity and stimulus. Remember though, no matter what you choose in your experience in this physical world you live in, God loves you.

You are not living in the physical reality of Earth by accident. Souls do not forget who they are and then fall from grace into a world of matter because of that forgetting. God did not put you on Earth saying: stay here and only after lifetimes of hard work you may finally earn the right to leave this physical world to exist at last in the spirit realm. God proclaims you infinite beings of divine love and divine abilities. He gives you this world as a choice. You may choose to be in it to experience yourself in such a way that you are opened to the fullest understanding of what he is and of what you are. You will stay only so long as you wish, and you will never be alone on your journey into the physical, for God's emissaries will assist you at all times. The choice is always yours, and you will always be allowed to choose without interference. Those in the spirit realm send you love and light in every moment of your chosen journey.

4

REINCARNATION:
A SPIRITUAL JOURNEY

You are on a spiritual journey. Although you travel the physical world, you are a being following the cadence of a higher energy. This energy is spiritual energy, the energy of God, which is universal in nature. This energy is not confined to the world of matter, nor is it limited by physical laws; rather it traverses the spheres. It is a very powerful energy and this energy is what you are. You came into being as high-level unlimited universal energy. It was only when you chose to encapsulate in a body in a world of matter that you became a being of limits. In the spirit world, you were a soul not limited by a body, but only limited by the soul's inability to fully comprehend itself as an unlimited being.

In order to understand itself as unlimited, the soul begins an expansion process. In that expansion, the boundaries of the limiting perceptions are pushed further and further away, and the soul begins to develop an expanded truer awareness of itself. To learn about being unlimited, the soul incarnates on Earth, a world of limits.

The spiritual journey and the physical life journey are one and the same; they are the soul's journey. When the soul takes on this journey, it is entering into a process of transformation that may take, in the measure of your time, a very long time. Many souls experience hundreds, even thousands of lives. This is the method they employ for the transformation of the soul, from one that possesses all knowledge but is unaware of it, to one that is aware and functioning at a very high level. Because of this process, humans in the physical reality have many experiences that provide the soul with opportunities for awareness. However, it also provides an opportunity for the human personality to grow in awareness. The soul is a constant in your physical reality. It will continue to participate in every experience that unfolds in each of your lives, and it is always the energy by which you are part of the spirit world.

As you choose experiences, you have an opportunity for those unfolding events to stimulate growth. Experiences in one life may affect your soul in a particular manner, which may lead to further exploration and development of that theme in another life, and yet another. Extrapolated from the series of interrelated experiences over lifetimes is the understanding that brings expanded awareness.

Karma is the effect past lives may have on the present. However, karma is not a law that creates your present reality as a result of experience from your incarnated past. Present life experience is usually connected to past life experience; but that is because free will allows the soul to choose to further explore particular experiences. Never is a soul assigned a life experience as a punishment or reward for past deeds. Do not get caught up in believing that karma is an avenue of punishment or a tool for judgment. You choose whatever you choose, at the soul level, because that is what will enhance and facilitate your expanding awareness.

Should a soul choose to follow through on a previous life experience, messages about the repeated experience begin surfacing in consciousness. Sent from the soul level, these messages are about healing. To heal is to repair or correct a situation which causes distress and imperils well-being. In healing, you bring into focus the situation creating distress. You gain the opportunity to examine it and understand it. In the understanding, you are then able to release and restructure the situation to create a harmony and balance that leads to a higher level of awareness. As a spiritual being and a physical being, you not only expand the awareness of the soul, but also expand the awareness of the physical being. This allows for you to create a physical life more harmonious with reality. It produces an ease of functioning that supersedes harsh difficulties and more readily ensures a life of productivity and peace.

Reality, as a perception of the physical self and as a perception of the soul self, is not always a harmonious view. It is in the cooperative venture of existing in the physical that the perception of reality is transformed through expanded sight. The combined sight of the inner and outer eye gives clarity to what is seen. That combined vision, supported through awareness, is an expanded perception that encompasses all the abilities of a being. A soul and physical self with expanding awareness perceives what the whole self is, and what it can mean to live life from the knowledge of the whole self, rather than just from the view of the ego-oriented physical self. When awareness is expanded through dual sight, the perception of reality is changed. Perception is expanded and is more aware. Understanding is more readily achieved, and reactions are more loving, compassionate, and on the mark in their ability to produce a desired effect. You move in a self-empowered way, confident, at ease, and at a comfortable pace with all events of life. You do not become a victim, because when you perceive and act from a point of soul awareness, you are aware of what is happening and are able to be an empowered participant rather than one who, without awareness, becomes a victim of circumstances.

Healing is recognizing and changing what needs to be changed in order to move in a self-directed way to a point of understanding. Through understanding, the path is smoother, the light is brighter, and the way is clear. In this focus, you are able to realize your highest potential and move through life in peace and joy. This movement through life is a dance resonating with love and acceptance that will transform your life.

5

ENERGY

The world you live in is a world of matter, but matter is created of energy. It is nothing more than energy slowed down and shaped into form. It is the tangible created to provide structure and continuity in order for events to have meaning and results.

In the world of spirit time does not exist, as from our point of view sequencing is unnecessary. Without a time structure, all events may appear random; however, with our expanded perception we are able to understand each event and its impact on the soul's evolvement. In the spirit world we exist within a world of pure energy where matter can and may be created, but is not required for continued experience.

Earth, on the other hand, is a world of matter, and without form created from energy it would move back into the realm of nonphysical existence. It would be absorbed into the universe. Many would fear this ending as punishment for the perceived non-evolvement of humankind, but that is not the case. Earth was not created as a testing ground or proving ground, nor was it created to be an experimental energy process. Earth was created to *be*, and therefore it will be. It has, much the same as you, free will. It exists within its structured environmental systems and within the physical universe by virtue of the physical laws that govern it. Earth was created as a place of experience, and it will sustain itself as long as desired because it is created of energy. Energy ever flexible, ever expanding, ever undulating with awareness, cannot be destroyed. It can, however, be altered, disrupted, and diminished. Yet, it can also be repaired and enhanced. It is capable of surviving whatever it chooses.

The allegories through the ages, of Mother Earth and spaceship Earth, are well founded. Your body is your mother providing you a home and nurturance. Your body, a living organism, is also your spaceship, a craft, a functioning ship within which the soul travels and experiences the unknown. As you are, Earth is; a mother whose energy received you, her children, and her existence has nurtured you and allowed you to experience. Earth is also a most impressive spaceship, a living organism that makes its way through infinity with you, her passengers who are magnificent beings of energy.

Because you are energy, you are affected by energy and you affect energy. The world has been limited by an intolerance of this truth, and as a result, humankind in its supposed sophisticated evolvement has moved away from recognition of this truth as powerful information.

Energy is what you are and, therefore, your greatest works will be done when you accept the capability that energy has to enhance your life experience. This enhancement, while experienced at the core level of each being, can be used to affect the energy of Earth. The experience of Mother Earth parallels that of Earth humans. If you harm yourself, or harm others, you harm the Mother. If you love and honor yourself and others, you will then love and honor the Mother.

Energy in its most powerful form is thought. Thought is the most powerful force in the universe. That is the simplest of truths, yet the most profound. Thought is energy awareness and the highest-level energy existent is the soul. Not the human soul, nor any soul encapsulated in any particular physical body, but just, very simply, *the* soul. As the soul is an aspect of the original soul of God, it is fully capable of generating and producing energy through thought. The word "thought" comes closest to describing the energy-producing process of the soul. I caution you, though, that words and definitions are limiting. Therefore, when you contemplate the word "thought," and the process of creating through thought, contemplate with your soul and your emotions and let them soar so that you will feel what thought truly is.

Energy varies, and it exists in many forms to create a vast repertoire of possibilities for universal experience, as well as physical experience. The thought that creates the energy also determines what the energy is. God created you from thought, in love, as a replica of himself. Each soul is unique and the energy unalterable. While unalterable from the original, enhancement and expansion are possible. This expansion and enhancement process is the energy reproducing process the soul undertakes when it begins its choices for experience. Each choice is a thought that is energy. The energy produced by thought affects not only the self, but also that to which the energy is directed. What that energy is, is determined by the creator that produced that energy.

It is important to know, however, that a soul cannot create another soul with thought. This is where you are different from God. God is the source of the highest-level energy. It is only from that Source that a soul can be created. This is what makes us different from our creator. God is the only creator of souls. God created in one moment all souls now in existence. None have been created since that initial thought, when existence and awareness were born through the love of God. God could expand his thought to create new souls, but at this time that is not occurring.

As beings of energy, the only thing that can truly affect us is energy. Energy enhances and diminishes, depending upon how we perceive it, use it and react to it. Emotions are energy that produce unrestricted reaction and thus unrestricted choice of how to respond. When you experience many different emotions, you find yourself responding and reacting to a whole spectrum of energy that runs from high level, positive, enriching energy to low level, draining negative energy. The way in which you respond to the energy is influenced by personal experience and the physical history of the soul.

A soul experiencing lifetimes of victimization will often be a physical being sensitized to victimization, be it real or imagined. As a result, aggressive action by another, with or without malice, is experienced in a response created of low level, negative, energy. This response stimulates thoughts of fear, anger, and revenge. These energy responses have the effect of locking one into a negative energy mode and can lead one into a cycle of low-level energy responses. This attracts like energy, which is, of course, negative energy.

Low level means denser energy. It is thick, heavy, and clouded and allows little room for light. Emotionally, it feels heavy. Physically, it feels heavy, lethargic, and fatiguing. The soul is high-level energy, and when encountering opposite or unlike energy it can cause concern for the soul.

In many cases, these experiences can be a springboard to learning if the soul and consciousness recognize the presence of energy unlike itself and creates, through thought, energy that is high level and infused with Godlike energy.

This is why white light energy is such a wonderful visualization. It is pure, clean, light, and airy. It is an infusion of the God energy, to protect, to enhance, and help the soul and consciousness move to a more positive energy level. This is why positive energy affirmations of love and well-being work. Repeated and visualized, they create through thought a positive high-level energy at the soul level. This process brings the energy of God into existence within your physical body and serves to enhance, expand, and bless your entire being. In this process, you move yourself into a higher vibrational energy. You are then able to project to Mother Earth and others a more healthful, loving, and expanded level of light-filled energy. You then co-create not only yourself, but also Mother Earth.

Energy is also the source of your physical well-being. Your human bodies, while falling within a natural order of evolution that means their inevitable demise—which I will say fits perfectly at this time within the scheme of the universe—often suffer prematurely and needlessly because of energy disturbances. As people understand more fully the nature of themselves and energy they will be able to sustain the human body in a very natural, gentle, and loving way and when it is time to depart this reality of the physical, the soul will simply exit, and the body will go into its last sleep and merely become the organic matter that it is. While that is not the norm now, it appears very likely that it will become so in the spiritual and physical evolution of Earth and its people.

Disease is a disturbance of energy. If a disturbance goes undetected and untreated, it will result in a physical disorder or disease, which will eventually manifest profoundly enough to be detected. I will say that at this time, in the evolving history of humankind and Earth, there is a need for physical discomfort and ailments. This is one of the learning experiences that help to enhance awareness of the separateness of the human body and the soul residing within it. As well, it emphasizes the well-being that is physically created in a harmonious relationship between the soul and its physical self.

At this time being physical is an important part of the Earth experience. Therefore, there is playing out within the choices of souls the need to experience a full range of physical and mental limitations and handicaps. As time produces shifts in awareness, through evolving experience at a conscious and soul level, there will be less and less need to explore the limitations of the physical body. Souls at the time between lives will then not choose physical limitations, because it will be territory already explored. The physical and spiritual exploration of energy as a creator of physical disability, as well as a healer, will open consciousness to acceptance of energy as the basis of all matter. This awareness brings the understanding that illness and disability are merely experiential illusions that can be released.

How wonderfully well humankind advances its world and personal well-being. It may not seem so, but the steps are being taken. They may seem small, minute, and painfully slow, but remember, we are forever; time is not the point. Awareness is the point.

6

PHYSICAL AND SPIRITUAL EXPLORATION

In the beginning, God created the universe. The universe as you perceive it with your physical eyes is the sun, the moon, the stars, and planets. However, this universe is also made up of much that is unseen by your physical eyes. Just because it is not readily seen does not mean that it does not exist.

In the earliest days of humankind on Earth, contemplation was limited to that which could be perceived by the physical senses. However, time passed, and humans becoming accustomed to their surroundings grew comfortable with the familiar and through curiosity and thought expanded their horizons. Curiosity and contemplation led to the exploration that created greater avenues of existence for these people. Awareness led to a comfortable acceptance of the known and to an overwhelming desire to explore the unknown. This explorative drive within the human race is the physical manifestation of that deepest internal desire to understand the true self.

The physical exploration of your world and your universe will always lead you back to the spiritual exploration of yourself. A world created by God can never be fully understood until you view it from within the framework of spiritual awareness. When you allow yourself to understand your existence from this vantage point the Light will literally turn on within you, and you will be in awe of what you learn.

God made all souls the same; therefore, the ability to perceive from the soul level is inherent within everyone. However, there are those more open to accepting that humans are more than they appear to be and that life on Earth is only one dimension and one expression of existence. For those who are open to knowledge, growth is assured. Those not ready to be open will choose not to hear. That is not a grave error on their part, but merely an indication they have not yet heard what will satisfy the unacknowledged questions within them. When an answer is heard, the questions can be acknowledged.

This time on Earth is just as it was hundreds and thousands of years ago: an evolution of intelligence and awareness. As it is in ages past, it still is. Many scoff at that which is not tangibly provable; what cannot be seen, touched, heard, weighed, measured, dissected, and photographed cannot possibly exist. Just as people scorned the new world Columbus envisioned, many scorn the idea of spirit reality and the soul's influence in your physical life. I say to those who doubt: you are an intelligent spiritual being unlimited by the physical world; you are capable of ruling the stars.

7

EXPERIENCES

Once upon a time God smiled and created all that is. You, my friend, are part of all that is, and therefore you are a special and unique being, a manifestation of love. What you come to realize when you accept your own unique and special place in existence is that every person is uniquely identified in the mind of God. You come to awareness that all around you in every human body is a soul equipped to meet the challenge of the journey through physical and spiritual existence.

Because of choices made at the soul level, as well as at the conscious physical level, the illusion created on Earth is one of inequity. When a soul makes a choice for a particular physical experience it very carefully develops those circumstances that will guarantee specific developments in order to ensure the desired experience. Each soul makes decisions that lead to its highest unfolding. The highest unfolding is that experience that expands awareness and enhances the journey of the soul.

For example, one can be born into wealth, filled with desire for even greater wealth. Or, one can be born into wealth with a disdain for acquisition and a desire to experience life without wealth. One can be born into poverty with an intense craving for wealth and the perceived power of wealth. There are also those born into poverty who do not seem to notice their physical poverty, for they feel richness and security within themselves.

Some will choose to experience illness or disability. Some will even come into the world with impaired mental capabilities. There are those who choose situations that lead to abusive childhood experiences.

There are some who lead lives that seem charmed; nothing seems to ever go wrong, and productivity and success is their experience. Others often envy these people. In the experience of life people pity the poor, curse the rich, fear the ill, and ignore the impaired, all out of a need to find their own superiority and worth and to find relief from their feelings of inadequacy.

I am here to help you understand the true nature of yourself; that first, you are a soul and a soul is created by God. What appears to be, and what you physically feel yourself to be, is only an illusion. It is created by you at the soul level in order to have experience. Experience is the ultimate teacher. Experience is the ultimate path to understanding what a soul truly is and the part the soul plays in the creation of what you are.

As co-creator with God of this physical reality, you have provided yourself with a way to manifest and express thought, to follow through the thought process by living the thoughts and explorative ideas of your own soul. You are, in your physical form, a thought process of your own soul.

It is important to understand that all souls are a manifestation of God. All people, then, at the core are very much the same. You are no more and no less than another, just as you are no more and no less than the God who created you. In this realization, you will come to understand that the human experience is a high-level manifestation of God, and because of free will, you become the co-creator of not only your personal experience, but the human experience.

I urge you to be respectful of all people, for you are sisters and brothers; to respect one another is to respect yourself. The respect of which I speak includes also respecting the choices one has made. You may not like the choices another person has made, and there may even be times when it is necessary and appropriate for you to take action against those choices, but this does not mean you should not respect that soul's right to choose. This concept is one of great difficulty for people to understand; however, with experience and awareness this understanding can come.

Do not be dismayed or angered by this concept, but allow it to sit within you and it will become clearer to you. You might look at it more comfortably this way: God's greatest gift to humankind is free will: the ability to freely choose your path and experience. How can you truly love, accept, and appreciate what you are unless you have the choice of what you will be? In that gift of free will, God imposed no restrictions, no judgment. God accepts and respects all choices and as a recipient of this gift, you are respected by God in your choices. Humankind also has the capability of accepting and respecting the free-will choices of all people.

The situations that arise when individual choices interfere with the free will of another create experiential situations, which is the point of physical existence. Free will means each person may choose how to act or react to all situations, which means each person becomes the creator of their own reality. Whether a person displays positive actions or negative actions, you choose your reaction to them, and it is your choice, not their action, that shapes your experience of their actions.

A soul may choose to manifest a life experience in the body of a man who is a greedy and cunning person. This man, while unpleasant to be around, has not truly committed an act of physical and spiritual aggression until he actually interferes with another's free will. Those who appear to be victimized by this man may in actuality be people who have their own lessons to learn and because of their choices take on the role of the victim. A simple, yet complex, fundamental truth of the human experience is that not all events that occur are for the singular experience of one person. Most events that occur in life involve more than one soul and more than one lesson to be learned.

In the physical reality, ending the life of another person against their will is interference of free will. But there are those times when it is not interference with free will because at the soul level, this act is agreed upon by these two souls. However, because these events occur in the physical world they are handled according to societal mores and established laws. It is important to do so, because even in cooperative situations where souls have agreed to an act, the point of the experience is that it is occurring in the physical world where the actions and reactions must adhere to the human experience in order for learning to occur for them as well as others.

The crucifixion of Christ is an example of a very significant cooperative experience. For many reasons, it needed to unfold as it did. It was not a random event, but a high-level unfolding created by many souls in order to achieve an experience that would significantly impact and influence humans, forever challenging their choices.

Everyone at the soul level chooses and creates experiences that cause learning not only for the self, but for others. At the physical level, you have freedom to choose your response to the unfolding experience your soul has helped create. The soul self creates, the physical self reacts. Experience is explored and awareness grows. The soul self can then choose to recreate the experience again through other situations, and the physical self again reacts, but perhaps differently. Thus, experience is explored, understanding is expanded, and the soul self and the physical self become aware of one another.

8

SELF-REALIZATION

Sometimes in life you find yourself contemplating your purpose for being here in this place, at this time, in this particular physical body. Marvelous questions for you to ask, for they are signs of life! They are signs that you are alive at all levels of your being: the physical, the emotional, and the spiritual. Rejoice that you contemplate your purpose, and rejoice even more, for the answers are within you. You are not just a tiny speck in the infiniteness of all that is, you are a part of it. For this, rejoice.

To the question of your purpose, I give this answer: your purpose is merely to be. Your purpose is to exist, to experience, to come to understanding, awareness, and enlightenment. You entered into this physical life to learn more about yourself, your soul self. You chose to do this, to come here to learn, because otherwise you would not be here, for no one would ever force you to be here against your will.

To be here is to experience, and to experience is to learn. Learning may not be perceived at the physical level, but understand that learning does take place at the soul level whether the conscious physical self perceives the learning or not. You cannot unconsciously hinder yourself into a state of non-evolvement, for the soul grows and expands without the participation of physical consciousness. However, think of the strides that can be made in the process of the soul's growth when the soul self and the physical self are working in concert.

Your brain is an amazing storehouse of energy that is capable of perceiving the self as a multidimensional being. A soul self and a conscious physical self, working in concert, are unlimited in their ability to enhance growth through a heightened state of awareness. Such a state of sensitivity gives you an expanded opportunity for understanding the many facets of each experiential situation. In the cooperation between the soul self and the physical self, you do not see with just your physical eyes, you see also with the inner eye, which allows you greater awareness of the unfolding situation. Experience framed in this way enhances learning, because your awareness is not limited to just the perceptions of the physical self.

In life, your experiences test the boundaries of the physical. The stress of these experiences stimulates a longing for explanation that becomes the catalyst for the internal search for meaning. Once that search begins, the soul self and physical self are engaged. This is the experience that typically leads to the initial realization, consciously or unconsciously, that you are more than just a physical being. From that point on, there is no returning to a state of disconnection with your soul.

The realization that you are more than just a conscious mind in a physical body is a breakthrough event. For some people it occurs when they feel God's light and love in a near-death experience. Others experience such profound pain and despair, and feel so removed from hope, that they fall through their own internal darkness into God's light within them. In that falling they feel God and come to realize they are more than their sadness and pain. Some people come to know God through creative expression, such as art, music, or writing. Whether they are the creator of it, or the appreciator of it, they feel the inspiration for the creation comes from a deep inner place that is connected to something more spiritual, something beyond the confines of the conscious mind.

When you meet and acknowledge your soul, you are meeting the aspect of God that is you. The breakthrough experiences may vary, but for each person there can be such an experience. I refer to it as the awakening. The choice of what to do with that experience is yours.

9

EMOTIONAL ENERGY—
EMOTIONAL HEALING

Because a soul must accumulate experience to enhance growth, experience is to the soul as food is to the body. The soul enters most life adventures with a willingness to experience that which is going to facilitate its growth. Encapsulated within the body, the soul is a participant in the physical experience through the higher self, and the sensory and motor functions of the brain. Its tool for involvement is emotion.

Emotions are energy reactions which give meaning to experiences and cause them to be imprinted in memory. This is why experiences devoid of emotion can be hard to remember. But in some cases, if the emotions of an event are too painful, they may be separated from the experience. Because emotions are energy they cannot be destroyed; therefore, in those circumstances the emotions are internally buried. When this is done, the record of the event surrounding the emotion is also buried, which means there is no conscious memory of it. The events buried with the emotions may be forgotten or lost, but they are never destroyed. Unfortunately, internally buried emotions can continue to cause distress for a person at the conscious level and also interfere with the soul's ability to expand its awareness. To promote health, well-being and wholeness, it is important to release negative emotional energy from the body as well as the soul. This is one of the more important tenets of healing.

Emotional energy either enhances the light or obscures or diminishes the connection to the light. Because souls were created from light energy, they are only compatible with energy containing light imbued qualities. Emotions that evoke feelings of love and joy, and create an inner sense of peace and hope and the recognition of self-value, are light filled and resonate with the soul. These emotions honor the self and others and reflect God's love into the world. They enhance the soul and your experience through self-perception of light in yourself and in others.

To live in this physical world is to live within a realm of unlimited emotionality. Emotional energy has evolved in this world of matter which has been created by dense energy. Because of its density, matter is light detracting, meaning it can obscure and isolate the internal light of each physical being. Positive emotional energy enhances that light within. Negative emotional energy takes away, and detracts by obscuring the internal light from consciousness. The light of your soul is always there, but when it is obscured it is difficult to expand it. For this understanding to be complete you must realize that in order for free will to be valid you must have the awareness of what the light creates and what it does not create. Each person must be afforded the opportunity to fully experience in a spontaneous way all emotions in order for that soul to know fully what its choices and opportunities are. Also, in this way opportunities become a realistic unfolding that offers validity to life experience. While life may be a stage, the soul in the physical is not merely an actor playing a preordained part, but more: a self-creator experiencing what it is in that moment.

Life experience, because of emotional experience, is very rich in contrasts and opportunities for personalized experience. From our vantage point in the spirit realm, we see clearly your advantages and opportunities, but we choose very carefully our words in dispensing personalized information, for in no way will we circumvent the opportunities unfolding and interfere with your choices. Earth is a very sacred place; it is the place in which you have chosen to honor your soul's desire for awakening, and in this physical experience are those circumstances and events you have chosen to utilize in your soul's quest to gain awareness. Expanding awareness is the path to awakening the soul. We would never interfere with such a holy process.

As you live through the events of this life, you undergo experiences that create many emotional responses and thus create and attract to you many varied emotional energies. You are born into a world of emotion where your physical body and spiritual body create emotions in reaction to the emotional energy encountered in the physical. You learn about emotions as you encounter experience. One cannot feel hate as an emotion until one encounters hate. The same with anger; it is only experienced as one encounters anger or other negative emotions. An individual more readily feels love, even if love is not given, because the energy of the soul is the energy of light and love. Every child born has within it high-level light energy which immediately connects with the energy of the soul. A child is naturally drawn to the wonderful emotions of the light. You can well imagine, then, the shock experienced by a child, as a being of light, if they are exposed to harsh, cruel trauma. It is sad that the child may experience this but it is an opportunity also for the soul to understand and explore many emotions, many choices.

It is difficult to explain the full scope of experience and its purpose and effect upon the soul if the explanation is limited to just one lifetime. Each life lived offers the impetus for the next life choice and so on. As the experiences of each life are recorded forever within the soul, so also are the emotional energies of each life. If you leave emotional energies which are light-detracting in an enveloped state within the human body, they will be held within the soul also. Long after the soul has left a physical life and physical body, the unresolved emotional issues can continue at the soul level to interfere with the energy of the light. Only when issues are recognized, examined, and healed is the negative energy removed to reveal the positive healing energy of the light. When the negative light-detracting emotion is released, you do not lose the memory of that experience; rather you reframe it within a structure of understanding which assigns to that experience emotions of peaceful acceptance.

Forgiveness is a releasing energy of healing. I don't mean the concept of forgiveness that calls for blind excusing, but rather the concept that calls for loving acceptance of what has been and the need to heal and release. True healing means self-examination and emotional release.

When you discover the need for healing, you take the step that leads to the replacement of a negative light-obscuring emotion with an emotion that enhances the light within you. This replacement comes quite easily and naturally once you are fully able to release the light-obscuring emotion. With the light clearly revealing the experience you can release and heal that situation, which will move you into peace. This process creates more light within you. As you move through incarnations, experiences that are negative in nature help expose the soul-level issues that need healing. As you recognize these issues and work to heal them, you enhance your soul's ability to expand into greater awareness. The more conscious work you do in each life to heal yourself of emotions that limit your inner awareness, the greater is your soul's opportunity to choose experiences uninfluenced by unhealed situations. The more that is resolved consciously in this life, the less you will take with you into another life.

In a healed state the soul's awareness is keener, decision-making is much easier and life is not such struggle. In this time, this place, this life, your soul chose to be you because of who and what you have been before. This life, while it does stand alone, is connected to the history of your soul. What you are now is important. You are the process by which the soul grows and heals. In this expansive process the accumulation of energy makes you what you are, and at the core of all that energy that you are is that pure energy of God's loving light.

10

THE PHYSICAL SELF AND THE SPIRITUAL SELF

My hope is that the information I offer will lead to the expansion of your awareness in this lifetime; that you will gain greater understanding of yourself and your relationship to all that is.

The truth is that you are a being of love, capable of accepting the knowledge the universe offers to help you open to God's light and love.

I am here to offer insight and suggestions to help you in your journey through this life. I explain this information as best I can so that you will be able to gain knowledge to assist yourself in your journey. As you move along your path, you will become open to newer and more expansive information. As you are personally ready to step into expanded awareness, you will find the information and guidance will be there for you; it will make sense to you, it will strike a chord and your heart will respond.

Your spiritual self is that part of your physical being that I refer to as your intangible self. It cannot be seen or touched, yet it is very real. Your physical self can be seen and touched, therefore it is tangible. You live in a world of matter that is created for both your physical self and your spiritual self. However, in its structure it is more similar to the physical self because it is tangible. In your relationship with this physical world, you forget that the intangible self, the spiritual self, is actually the truest self. It is the self that will exist forever, long after the physical self has been exhausted and expired. The physical body has been created as the vehicle for the soul to utilize in its quest for experience, and each experience on Earth is bounded by the limitations of Earth and its inherent natural laws. Therefore, life has to end, creating a cycle of beginnings and endings. Because of this, the soul experiences limits. This restrictive, limited time frame creates the structure and harmony within which the experience can take on meaning.

Because Earth can be a harsh environment to exist within, the human body was imbued with particular attributes to ensure its survival and continued evolution so that it could be sturdy and strong enough to support the high-level energy of the soul. Therefore, there are parts of you more aligned with your physical self that are only activated when the body is born and begins life. It is important to understand that although these aspects are part of the physical body, they do have an effect on the soul and the functioning of the whole self. Your spiritual self is that part of you born into the physical world with the entrance of the soul into the physical body. The engagement of the physical self and the spiritual self creates a body able to live and function in the Earth reality.

It is important that all parts of the being—the physical and the spiritual—work in harmony to gain the experience that ensures the growth and expansion of the soul. As I describe the parts of the physical and spiritual being, you will see that harmony is not always readily achieved. While harmony is highly desired, it is the temporary lack of it that helps to create some of the experiences which the soul needs for its growth.

11

∞

THE KEY

(THE ENERGY POINT)

The Key, also referred to as the energy point, is a part of your physical body. It is present even before the soul enters into the body; it is the energy which causes the body to develop from a single cell and expand itself into the completed human form. The Key is that spark of energy within the physical that activates the vital physical functioning of the whole body.

The energy point is present at conception, created by the unification of the female egg and the male sperm. All that exists is created of energy. Matter is nothing more than energy in various degrees of density taking form. However, as the human is biologically conceived, the human parent's energy ignites the spark of energy that encapsulates within the fertilized egg. That high-level energy supports fetal development. In order for the human body to survive outside of its parental womb, it must have the presence of the soul, for the soul is the even higher level of energy, which assures the functioning of all aspects of the being. The Key energy keeps the fetal body growing and developing to the point where a soul enters, which then assures the further development of the whole being.

Upon entry into the unborn physical body, the soul engages the Key/energy point. Their union is the ignition, the beginning of fuller expression as a viable functioning being. The engagement of the key and the soul ignites the mental processes of the physical being; it is when the physical body moves from a fetal state to the human state. The fetal body can exist without a soul in it, but to have potential for developing into a viable human body the energy point must be present. If fertilization occurs and an energy point is not developed, the egg will not continue to expand and will spontaneously abort. When the Key is present, the soul will enter the fetal body, infusing it with high-level energy; thus the ignition is sparked and life, in the fullest sense of the word, begins.

The human body cannot come into existence without the Key, and it cannot be born and begin life without the soul. The person cannot survive without both of them present. There are situations, however, in which the body can temporarily survive as a physical shell even when vacated by either the soul or energy point, but not both. For example, a being in a deep state of unconsciousness such as a coma is often a physical body where the Key/energy point is present and the soul departed. Rarely can you know for certain what the situation is, but usually it is the soul that is gone, for it is the soul that activates on-going conscious intellectual functioning.

In a near death experience where one is declared clinically dead yet regains consciousness, it is usually the Key/energy point that has vacated the body simulating the experience of death. Rarely, in this kind of experience does the soul leave the body and if it should, typically it will not return, which means death occurs. All of this can be explained in greater detail, but for the purpose of this body of information, this cursory information is to give you more awareness of the physical body and spiritual body as two separate aspects of yourself that work together.

The Key/energy point has some awareness of the soul. Remember, the Key, as a part of the created physical body, has not existed before, unlike the soul. Therefore, the Key does not have awareness of itself at all. However, at the point where the soul energy and Key energy engage, the Key has an awakening and can then, to some degree, perceive itself as something. As a result of the energy exchange between the two, the Key is also able to recognize the presence and whereabouts of the soul and to have access to the information of the soul.

Keys respond to soul energy in different ways. While many are comfortably drawn to the soul, others, out of fear or confusion, will stay away from the soul. The Key does not have to understand and accept the soul in order for life to continue. After the initial engagement, the soul and Key can separate and go their separate ways within the body. However, there are times when it is important for the Key to have understanding and awareness. A critical example of that is when an ego state forms itself around the Key. Ego states are often attracted to the energy of the Key and may attach to it and even encapsulate it. This interference with the Key limits the free flow of its energy, which can negatively impact the conscious life of the person. The issue of an ego state surrounding a Key is significant when one is working with emotional and physical healing.

12

∞
THE SOUL AND THE HIGHER SELF

In creating the human body to provide a physical vehicle for the soul's experience, it was realized a person would need access to the soul and the information it contains. For this purpose, your higher self exists. The higher self is a connecting link between the physical self and the soul.

The higher self is a part of your soul and is not separate from you. It is the part of yourself connected with the spirit world, and it serves as your spiritual advisor. The higher self is not the soul; it is an extension of the soul's energy that is indigenous to the particular lifetime that you are living.

The soul is more than a higher self, for it concentrates not on one life, but on many. Although the soul is currently residing within this one body, it is actually without boundary in this physical life and continues to exist multi-dimensionally.

The higher self is the aspect of your soul that grounds itself in the present physical existence and takes its basis for reality from this particular life. The higher self focuses itself in the present life and connects you to the soul and universe as it relates to and benefits this present life. In this way, the higher self is able to focus in on those experiential needs that are most important to this life.

When the Key/energy point and soul unite, the higher self is energized, and it is activated and imprinted with the particular physical life being lived. Each life experience your soul has undertaken has its own higher self. The higher self of this life is not the higher self of your last life, nor will it be the higher self of your next incarnated life. Each life incarnation has as its caretaker, or overseer, a higher self of its own. In this way, as all experience is recorded in the soul, it is recorded compartmentally under the energy of each higher self.

The higher self is the highest form of uniquely activated energy within your physical body, and every experience of this life is encoded and imprinted with the same energy identification as the higher self. Higher self energy is the root energy of each life a soul lives. This root energy is unique and unlike

31

the energy of other lives and other higher selves. In this way, with like energy attracting like, you are able to have shape and form and identifiable history within a soul that is not subject to the structure of time. Information within the soul is not structured by time sequencing. The order is created by energy encoding. By matching experiential energy to higher self energy, one is able to recreate the personal experience of a physically manifested soul in a particular lifetime. It is quite simple and effective.

Your soul is what you are and will always be, long after you leave this life (or any life) and long after you leave the cycle of physical life reincarnation. The soul is a sleeping giant—a body of energy with potential not fully tapped and as yet not fully understood or examined from the point of view of your physical perception. The potential of the soul as manifested in the physical has yet to be fully explored. The soul's experience is of its own making, and this cycle of birth and death in the Earth plane existence is but one facet of the total experience available to the soul. While your consciousness seems to perceive only one reality, I assure you that your soul has connection with and interaction in other dimensions even as you experience this life.

Your higher self has some awareness of this multi-dimensional connection and can affirm this for you. However, the focus of your higher self is to be grounded in this physical body, this personality, this experience, so that comprehension and continuity are not lost or interfered with. Life experience in the physical is after all, quite important. Were it not, you would not be here.

The time is coming when, in the physical, humans will connect with their soul, and conscious physical awareness will include soul awareness. This is experienced somewhat, but only slightly, at the time between life incarnations when one exists within the spirit realm. Those journeys into the spirit world are sojourns for rest and reflection, a time to ensure that choices for future physical experiences are on the path for the highest good. During these interludes in the spirit realm, the soul—the sleeping giant—is still slumbering.

The awakening is the movement of the soul into oneness with itself, the point when enlightenment brings full recognition of unlimitedness and the soul fully awakens and claims its power. At this point, the soul moves into a level of existence that is absolutely all encompassing, all knowing, and all-powerful.

As you enhance your physical experience by expanding conscious exploration and understanding, you enhance the ability of your soul to recognize itself and its true nature. It is experience, exploration, and expansion that lead the soul to total awakening. When the soul reaches the point of full awareness it will then begin a new journey. This journey is seldom spoken of, for it is not one carried out in the Earth plane, but rather in other places in other ways.

13

∞

THE HUMAN MIND

(THE CONSCIOUS, UNCONSCIOUS, INNER MIND, AND WILL)

As people existing in a world of challenges, it is important to live fully in your experience. To assist you in doing this, available to you is past life history that can help you understand within a larger framework why some of these experiences are occurring.

The human mind, comprised of various important parts, is energy within brain energy. The parts of the mind that assist in accessing past life history and in recording present life history are the conscious mind, unconscious mind, the inner mind and the will.

The Conscious and Unconscious Minds

Through your conscious mind you have awareness and experience of the physical reality. Humans, through interaction with others, act and react to become the creators of reality. Consciousness is the "you" that presents to the world, the personality that others become familiar with and perceive as you.

Your unconsciousness is a storehouse, a repository of information gathered from all experiences in your present life. The unconscious is the storage basement where no one often goes; it is the place where everything you do not remember is stored.

The unconscious is often perceived as an extremely intelligent part of the self. However, while the unconscious has the ability to store information and to react to information, it does not create reality.

Genius lies with the creator. It is your soul and your conscious self that are the creators. The unconscious self is the connector between the soul and the conscious self.

The soul is both the core of your being and the storehouse of your history. As the soul strives to gain greater connection with the consciousness of the physical self, it sends into the unconscious mind information about who you are and your relationship to God. These are the initial spiritual stirrings that awaken as you grow and mature and have cognizant recognition of yourself as a person. The soul sends information into the unconscious mind, which is part of the physical body, where it can then migrate into the conscious mind for recognition and examination.

The unconscious mind does not know whether the information passing through it to consciousness is past life or present life information. The function of the unconscious is not to discriminate or judge, but to allow information to pass through to consciousness. This can be done quite easily if there are no ego states preventing that information from proceeding to a conscious level. Remember, ego selves in the unconscious mind are created by the ego to protect consciousness. Therefore, any information stored in unconsciousness can be blocked from moving into consciousness by these ego states. Any information passing into the unconscious mind from the soul can be perceived by the ego states as unknown and threatening, so its passage into consciousness can be blocked by the ego states as well. A spiritual journey becomes a healing journey when emotional healing of the physical being is necessary in order to make an unhindered connection with your soul. The healing opens you to greater experience through expanded awareness of yourself and your spiritual relationship with all that exists in both the physical and spiritual realms.

While present life history is recorded in the unconscious mind, it is also recorded in the soul. Therefore, when the physical body ceases to function and thus, the subconscious ceases to exist, there is no interruption of history as it is also recorded in the soul, which exists forever.

The history of the soul is the information that helps you provide the framework from which you create your reality. Through your experiences in the physical you piece together the never-ending story of your soul. Your history is always significant in your experience of the present.

The unconscious mind records and transmits to the soul your history and your responses to your history. It becomes the receiver that transmits from the physical to the soul and is also the transmitter that broadcasts from the soul to consciousness. It helps the experiences make the transition from one level of awareness to the other.

The Inner Mind

The inner mind is a switching station. It is an observer and knows what level of functioning is going on within a being. Like the unconscious mind, it is not a creator, yet is it not a reactor as the unconscious is; it is more a reporter of the current status within. Devoid of emotion, it is not truly a spiritual aspect of the self and neither is it truly a physical aspect. Rather it is a combined energy of the physical and spiritual that becomes a neutral point of observation. It presents a view that is neither a spiritual point of view nor a physical point of view; it is just a view. Its existence is advantageous when you need a neutral observer, particularly in the process of inner healing. While most people are not aware of this part of themselves, it is a helpful part should it be needed.

The Will

The will is an energy created of both physical and spiritual energy, which can receive information and guidance from the soul level. It can then choose how it will act upon situations unfolding in the physical reality, as well as those occurring at the soul level. The will can influence consciousness and can be influenced by consciousness. It can also be influenced by the soul. The will can indirectly influence the soul through the choices it makes at the unconscious level and by the choices consciousness makes due to the influence of the will.

The will's purpose is multifaceted and seems to be dictated somewhat by the soul's chosen direction for a particular life. It wields a certain amount of power. Its purpose is to become the counterbalance between the soul self and the physical self. As the soul and physical self go back and forth in an attempt to understand and gain awareness of each other, the will also gains a perspective of the whole. When the will finally understands the needs of the soul and the physical being, it will attempt to be a harmonious point between the two to assist in a productive and peaceful balance.

You are not a random energy. You are created very exquisitely, a finely tuned machine, every part vitally important. Capable of high level functioning, this human machine is also a spiritual marvel, a wonder of God's most beautiful universe.

14

EGO

Ego, an often-maligned part of your being, is essential for the survival of the body. Humans are unique in their ability to emotionally feel and experience; they are very sensitive, and never is this sensitivity as acute as in the very early years of life. Life experience in the physical world can often be brutal, and the pain that causes can annihilate a person. The body, created for great purpose, was also created with a safety valve, a way to protect the being from devastating emotional and physical pain that could cause the loss of will to live.

That safety valve is the ego. At the first activation of fear and pain, the ego will set into motion whatever internal defenses are necessary to shield one from the effects of painful trauma. The ego is a valued and necessary friend, yet a friend who in protecting begins the process that can break down the whole being. One way the ego protects is in isolating and encapsulating the event that caused emotional distress, separating that experience from the whole self. This is a very effective means of protection, but it also creates its own problems. Experience is recorded in memory. Therefore, to isolate the event and remove it from conscious memory means also isolating the part of the self that holds the memory.

This loss of memory of some specific events, typically traumatic events, is identified by some health care professionals as dissociative disorder. Ego states are those parts of the self that separate from consciousness along with the memory. In many ways, that part of the self, the ego state, is like a miniature person locked away in the isolated experience that becomes its world. While the rest of the self may be free of that experience and, in many cases, even free of the memory of it, that part of the self is still there encapsulated within it, still feeling the pain and fear.

The perception is that to save the self, the part must be sacrificed. The whole self is what is necessary for complete awareness and the encapsulation of ego selves is very depleting to the abilities and functioning of the being. In some cases, ego states continue in their experience without detection by the conscious self. However, I assure you that in spite of a lack of conscious awareness of these ego states, there is an ongoing influence upon the conscious being by these ego state selves. This influence is usually counterproductive to good mental, emotional, and physical health.

The goal in developing greater understanding of the ego is to realize that while the ego is a very necessary and vital component of the human body, it can, by virtue of its function, create havoc and problems. The solution to this problem is not to rid the being of the ego, but to educate and befriend the ego in order to have it assist you in a fully cognizant way. The ego is also a warning device that can alert you to the issues in your life that need your attention. The ego becomes the yardstick to measure where you were and where you are. This assists your passage into new understanding with awareness of the passage and of the internal changes taking place. The ego reflects unconscious beliefs to consciousness, exposing the negative and fearful beliefs that need to be resolved in order to move to expand consciousness. I assure you, there is not a person born who does not go through some experience requiring the protection of the ego. What the ego causes to happen because of its protective measures, it is also able to undo once it understands the problem and the ability of the whole self to correct and heal that problem.

How do you engage the ego and make a friend of it? How do you have it understand and assist in the healing process? Simply put, you introduce the ego to the soul and higher self. The ego does not know you have a soul, much less a higher self. The ego perceives only the tangibles; therefore, it will in many cases resist the concept of soul, because the ego takes seriously its responsibilities and perceives itself as the one in charge. However, the ego has the ability to change its perception.

15

∞
EXPANDED AWARENESS

(THOUGHT AND INTUITION)

As a being of light, you have great capabilities and as you grow in your knowledge of yourself, you will become more attuned to your abilities. The greatest abilities of the physical being are being able to think, perceive, conceptualize, question, and be curious. Thinking has nothing to do with intelligence. Intelligence is the brain's ability to absorb and disseminate acquired information. What I speak of is *thought*, the ability to energize existence into conceptual expression and create through actions an expression of ideas and inherent knowledge. Thoughts are given to you by no one. You create your own thoughts in response to the thoughts of others.

Thought is the energy that links us together; it is the interactive fiber of this vast universe. It is the most powerful force in the universe. It is what creates our existence and causes it to continue. Thought is the spark that lit the flame and the fire that keeps burning.

There are many topics of interest to people seeking to understand, but without thought, there would not be the desire to explore these topics. Thought provides the impetus to explore and to continue exploring where there appear to be boundaries. It is the flame that feeds upon itself, never extinguished as it both consumes and ignites, burning ever stronger and brighter.

Thought aids humans in perceiving reality with expanded vision, which encourages perception beyond the physical senses. In life, you are constantly stimulated through your sensory perceptions, while at the soul level there is a different form of perception at work. Soul level perceiving has the potential to become more active at the physical level if one tunes into it. Perception from the soul level will help expand your reality in the physical to its maximum potential. It is the means by which you create a reaction to stimulus that is beyond the limited and restricted reactions of the human ego.

The key to this process is intuition. Intuition is an inner knowing that comes from the soul, which has access to unlimited sources of knowledge and to the loving assurance of all that is. In that pool of knowledge is the information that leads to expanded thought about any given situation. It leads also to viewing the situation within a framework that encompasses the unknown past, the unknown present, and the unknown future.

Going within to the expanded experience can offer you the peaceful insight and wisdom of knowing more than meets the human eye. With that knowing you are able to move back into the exterior world of the physical reality with the peace of greater understanding. A consciousness at peace can choose to react from an expanded point of view, to offer love and understanding to people and situations. With this internal knowledge, you have the ability to honor and respect a situation, to allow it to be, and to unfold. In doing so, you see the situation for more than the nuisance it may appear to be. It may feel like a nuisance, but with expanded awareness, the situation becomes an opportunity to learn.

As you move through life, you will come to realize that you are not at the mercy of people, elements, and circumstances. While all these may have an effect upon you, they do not create you. Rather, they enhance you by offering you the opportunity to make of a situation what you will. It can be anything you desire, but with expanded awareness and understanding, you are able to react in a creative and positive way. You have a key to creating for yourself a life enriched through knowledgeable experiencing heavily endowed with power. It is the power to learn, to expand knowledge of yourself as a physical personality and to be in tune with the spiritual nature of yourself, which affects your physical existence and the advancing awareness of your soul. God gave you these abilities and offers you opportunities to develop your physical being into a body of strength and knowledge and a soul of awareness and love.

Ponder upon your ability to think; it is neither a process of information attainment, nor the process of following the teachings of another. Thinking is the ability to process and compare acquired external information with your intuition, to then feel and know your relationship to that acquired information.

If someone tells you something, at some level you react to it. If the subject is one of significance, the energy of it will resonate deep within you, connecting with your intuitive energy. When attuned to this energy you transcend the smaller depiction of life and move into a larger-scale understanding of what is unfolding. This reactive process of the intuitive self, which is a part of the soul's activity, is a spiritual process.

As you become more open to the intuitive process, you become more adept at recognizing it and working with it. Should you learn to trust your intuition and follow its guidance, you will find your path smoother and your thoughts much clearer. Intuition is the power to see into the universe, to discern your place in it and your true relationship with all that is. With this knowledge, you become less limited, and are able to achieve and affect your life as you feel best enhances you and your experiences.

Intuition is a helper that gives you an edge in life if you listen to it. In order to hear this intuitive helper, you need only be open to listening and recognizing it. Many people are very aware of their intuition, but often refer to it as instinct, a gut feeling, or a knowing feeling. That is exactly what your intuition is: a knowing so strong, so resolute, that to deny it is a near impossibility. Many people, while they do not deny this process within themselves, do, nonetheless, deny its credence and disregard its message. These same people often wonder why things do not seem to go well for them in life, why there seem to be so many difficulties and obstacles. It is because they do not listen and heed their own intuition, the inner voice of high-level guidance.

Intuition is a process that is part of the higher self. The higher self is a part of the soul, and despite being encumbered within the physical body, it is in communication with the universe, with guides, and with all that is. Because of that connection, the higher self has knowledge and information to assist you in all situations. If you listen, and learn to trust and heed its messages, you will find it brings positive results because it is information for your highest good.

God did not ordain humankind to have difficulties, but in allowing free will, he allowed the chance for difficulty. He does, however, always offer guidance. The challenge of being in the human body is that its limits can obscure the direction to follow; intuition is God's way of guiding you.

God loves you and does not leave you without resources. As you only feel as great as you know yourself to be, God will do all to ensure you have every chance to realize your fullest potential. Yet, he will leave the choice to you as to whether or not you take advantage of your abilities. No choice is ever the wrong choice, but merely the right choice for you at that particular time.

If you have not already discovered your intuition, look for it. Throw caution to the wind, live recklessly for a moment, and follow the instinctive draw of the intuitive process. You will be most amazed and pleased with the results. Two points to consider: all results of following your intuition may not be immediately noticeable or recognizable, so be open to waiting to recognize the results of your intuitive choice; and, if you are one who is by nature a bit on the impulsive side, I advise you to discern between impulse and intuition. Give yourself a quiet time before reacting. If the notion to act upon this feeling goes away quickly and easily, then likely it was an impulse more characteristic of your physical nature. The intuitive action comes from the spiritual side of you and does not so readily and easily give way. Be open, trusting, and patient, and in your intuitive processing you will find yourself engaging a powerful and a trustworthy ally.

16

CREATING YOUR REALITY

It is you who give action and meaning to my thoughts and through your choices bring into your world the love and energy of which my words and thoughts are a part. You are the implementer of God's love and truth in the physical reality. I am merely the prompter, the one who reminds you of what you already know inside you. Thus, we work in concert, you and I, to establish the vision of truth as a reality on Earth.

You are not alone in your quest for truth. All over the world, people are on a quest for knowledge that will lead to an understanding of the existence and purpose of humankind. In your quest, you will find the tools for life enhancement: self-awareness and self-empowerment. When you are an aware, empowered person, you are an unlimited person, and in that state, you create your reality in a sound and healthful way.

People with whom I have worked often question my frequent referral to their ability to create their own reality. It is true that you create your reality by the way you react and think. When you come to understand that thought is the most powerful force in the universe, you have embraced the most powerful concept you can have about your being, whether in spirit form or physical form.

As you move through your experiences of life in the physical reality many events, situations, and people affect you. While it may be true that you cannot always prevent certain events from unfolding and affecting you, it is true that you can control your thoughts and thereby create your response and reaction to these events. This is creating your reality. If you think of a situation that you are in as one of loss and negativity, you create that perception of your reality.

If you think negatively, you will most definitely attract to yourself other negative energies. Please remember that like attracts like. If you consciously move to a level of awareness that helps you perceive from a more spiritually aligned viewing point, you will find your thoughts more positive and expanded, and thus you will perceive a reality that is more positive and expanded. Once again, you open yourself to attracting a like energy. Positive energy will attract more positive high-level energy experiences to you.

So simple, yet so complex; the key is to remember your perspective. If you view life on Earth as only a physical reality, then you limit your perspective and your ability to create. However, if you view this life on Earth as a spiritual unfolding in a physical reality, you will find yourself able to view all events in your life with expanded understanding.

With this spiritual perspective of yourself and all events affecting you, as well as others, you will find an enhanced ability to create your own high-level responses. In this way, you assist yourself in moving through your chosen physical experience with grace and ease. It creates knowing acceptance that is highly conducive to an inner peace that assists you in remaining open and receptive to the learning inherent in all your experiences.

I do not say this awareness is always easily maintained, for, after all, you live in a reality of many distractions. However, as you work to maintain your spiritual view you will find yourself getting to that place with greater and greater ease. The wonderful benefit of becoming aware of yourself as the creator of your experience is self-empowerment.

Self-empowerment is a magnificent and desired feeling; however, some have confused it with having power over someone or something. This is not what self-empowerment is. When people are unaware of their ability to create their own reality, they perceive that power lies in creating and controlling the lives of others. This perceived power is draining and will lead only to a feeling of emptiness, for true empowerment is not controlling others, but is in actualizing your ability to create.

I remind you that while you are a physical being, you are more importantly a spiritual being. To view yourself as only a physical body functioning because of the evolutionary process, or because God needed to command an army of souls on Earth, is not an accurate perspective of yourself. You are here at the behest of your soul to live in a reality that will help you understand yourself and your ability to create. Therefore, by remembering that you are a spiritual being, you give yourself an edge in understanding what you are, why you are here, and why you are having the particular personal experiences that you are having.

As you have this understanding of who you are, you are able to pass into and through all your experiences without kicking, screaming, and lamenting, but also without a passive, meek ambivalence. Instead, you move into and through all your experiences with awareness, eagerness, and a sense of participation, accomplishment, and completion. In this way you enrich, enhance, and enjoy your experiences of Earth existence.

I wish you a pleasant journey, and by that, I do not mean a life that is easy and without challenge, but rather a life full of all that you need to grow into your own power. I wish also that you do it with awareness that you are absolutely, unequivocally capable of doing all you need to do and want to do, and that you are also able to enjoy it.

17

SPIRITUAL ALIGNMENT

I, as a being of light, come to assist your personal quest for understanding. While you search and journey through this world of matter, you also journey through the world of your soul, which is, after all, the real you. You are not a physical being, be very clear about that. You are a spiritual being. A body of energy condensed into matter creates a body of matter. However, you are not this body; you are merely an inhabitant of it. You are a being of greater complexity than you can ever imagine. You embody the most profound, yet most simple of truths; you are a part of the God that created all that is.

Many people on Earth are limited by the fears of their ego, which aligns them more with their physical self than their spiritual self. In this alignment with the physical, people often define God in terms of the physical world. To do this limits the concept of God and the actuality of God in your life. When you limit the concept, you limit the experience of that concept to the boundaries you perceive.

When you perceive God from a point of the physical ego, you confine God within a limited perception. When instead you perceive God from soul awareness, through the conscious use of your intuitive higher self, you will then perceive God from the point of awareness from which God emanates, the energy source of all that is. Humans limiting perception to the physical reality limit their view and understanding of what God is and what humans are.

People often ask me what their life purpose is. At times, I can give them information that addresses that question, but what should not be lost in the focus on personal purpose is the knowledge that your true purpose is to experience: to live, to question, to answer, to teach yourself and teach others through being and experiencing in this very moment. That is all that is required to fulfill life's purpose. Just be. You do not have to fulfill any obligation. You have none, except for that which you may impose upon yourself. We here in the spirit realm know that existence is the purpose. Exist. Be and do. Grow, share, love, and explore. Be, and allow others to be.

Just as you would not wish imposition and unjustness thrust upon you, attempt not to impose it upon others. In a restricted view of each other, the imposition of limits sets into motion events that create a wave of oppression and fear, breeding negativity that creates itself over and over. Instead, offer to the world acceptance and tolerance. Offer love and high-level thinking. Use your physical brain to explore concepts from a spiritual perspective versus a physical perspective, and you will find your perception growing beyond that of a fearful and defensive ego. When you perceive from a spiritual awareness, you will discover your own innate ability to love more freely, and to accept and tolerate and work with those situations which previously caused you great difficulty. In this way, you open and expand yourself to be a loving emulation of God, rather than a limited, uninformed critic of the human condition.

18

JUDGMENT

I come to tell you that God is not judgmental. Judgment implies perception, but from God's point of view is not meant to imply action. God wishes for you to perceive and understand, but not to judge and take action upon that judgment. When you perceive without judgment you open yourself to greater concepts and ideas; you expand your knowledge and are able to recognize the many varied and creative expressions of experience.

To perceive the variety of experiential expressions and choose one over the other as your personal form of expression is not to imply that the one not chosen is inferior. You are here to experience, not to be the arbiter of right and wrong, for there is no right or wrong, but only experience and choices that propel that experience in one direction or another. For many people, however, there is a need to define the self as right or wrong in order to satisfy the ego's need for acceptance. In the ego's desire for acceptance is born the need to judge.

Judgment causes confusion for you. You wonder about the people who commit acts of harm upon another; are they to be left to run rampant in destructiveness? Of course not. To be nonjudgmental does not mean to be irresponsible in protecting the well-being of individuals. Rather, it means to act from the knowledge within you that is based in God's love, so all actions are from a point of knowledge and compassion and not from a point of fear and hostility. The person who harms another must be dealt with according to the laws prescribed, but it must be acknowledged that this individual, although acting out, is still a being of God, just as you are. You do not judge a being as right or wrong, but acknowledge that they have for their own reasons made choices to act outside the prescribed rules of society, and for that they must experience the consequences. This does not mean they are a wrong being or a right being; even God does not make that pronouncement.

Remember, your world was built upon one principal law: love one another as you love yourself. As humans have forgotten how to love the self, there has evolved avarice and greed, which has led to many violent acts. This does not mean that people are bad, only that people have forgotten to love. Laws made by humankind have been conceptually created to protect people, to ensure to some degree their safety and well-being. However, it is important to understand that sometimes even well-intentioned laws, if created in fear, create problems of their own.

Only when humankind is able to move back into the ultimate truth of love will fear of one another be replaced with love of one another. Following that is the dissolution of judgment that will occur when all feel the ultimate bond of love and compassion that connects us in our oneness with God. So be it.

19

ACCEPTANCE

As an infinite being, your experiences carry you through infinity to enhance the awareness of your soul. Through the experience of limitedness in the human body, you are able to examine the unlimitedness of the soul. Physical experience is sequenced within time so that it may have a coherent meaning that impacts your consciousness and the soul. The soul as energy is vast in its potential and capable of great awareness. However, initially it is closed. It is compact and dense, closed like a flower bud, and it is experience and expanding awareness that brings it into the beauty and understanding of what it is. A rosebud in its closed state does not recognize or understand its potential for full bloom. Yet, in its closed state it is all that it will be in full bloom. So it is with your soul—complete, perfect, the rose in bud. For the soul, experience and developing awareness through experience is what expands it into full bloom, into an understanding and awareness of what it truly is. Experience is the energy that nurtures and expands the soul, and just as all aspects of energy seek to sustain and nurture themselves, so does your soul.

In the spirit world, universal energy nurtures all souls, including those who have not yet begun their process of expansion to acquire awareness. But, at some point, the choice is made and the soul begins the journey to understanding, the journey to awakening.

When the soul is ready, the journey through the world of limits begins. At this point, as the soul leaves dormancy into activity, it is given an energy boost by the universe and it is cut loose—free to do as it will. The soul's energy is adjusted and synchronized with the energy vibration of the physical reality. When that adjustment takes place, the soul loses some awareness of what it is as it becomes more aligned with what is. That loss is sometimes called the "forgetting." As the soul enters the physical reality within a physical body, consciousness moves into the foreground as the physical manifestation of the soul. The body is a shell, the home, but the personality is the representation of the soul, the means by which it participates in this particular experience. This is how the soul acquires experience that will allow it to gain perspective of itself in relationship to emotions.

Over many lifetimes, a pattern evolves for each soul as it acquires experiences that affect not only subsequent life experience choices, but also the physical personality that manifests. The personality as representative of the soul will present those characteristics which are currently of primary importance to the soul. Those do not necessarily represent the soul's present level of evolvement, but rather represent the direction of growth to which the soul addresses itself.

It is very difficult from a physical viewpoint to establish the current status of a soul merely by the current physical status of the representative personality. What may seem to be in the physical is not necessarily the status of the soul, but more the creative endeavor of the soul to fully explore existence. Therefore, judgment of the soul behind the presenting personality is an assumptive task and can be most inaccurate. Your responsibility is not to judge the soul or the personality, but to view their experience and choose what part you will play in it.

Life experiences are for experience, nothing else. Experiences are not to punish you for previous life misdeeds. They are not for you to make amends. The lives you live, while tied to previous life experiences, stand alone in their ability to offer understanding and growth. To see someone as a helpless victim who evokes your greatest sympathy and concern, is to see one who has chosen that experience for any number of particular reasons. Therefore, you cannot assume to know why they are having such difficulties in their life. They may be exploring this role in order to contrast it against a previous life as an oppressive, dictatorial, controlling abusive person. Or they may have had many life experiences as a victim and are still choosing it in order to come to a healing awareness and understanding of victimization. It may be a role they have observed and wished to experience so that the soul could gain understanding and compassion. Or, perhaps, the choice was to be the victim to another soul's role of oppressor in order to create a cooperative learning experience.

The variations, the themes, the reasons are many, and to attempt to evaluate the progress of the soul through its current physical life status is quite futile. Acceptance of each life as it is manifested is important. You may, in the physical, not like nor agree with the many representative experiences, but they all have their validity. Just as your choices are highly regarded, so are the choices of all souls.

20

⊕

EVOLUTION

I am often asked questions about the evolution of man. Did man evolve from the monkey? I respond: did God not make the monkey and therefore not make man? God created all, but he did so in accordance with the physical laws of your world. These physical laws govern your planet, and as God planted the seeds with love, he allowed the seeds unhindered growth so they could evolve to become what they needed to be. Because souls must adapt to the lower density vibration of the physical world, the natural evolutionary process allowed for the creation of a physical body that is a safe and sure vehicle from which the soul can experience physical life to the fullest. The Creator allowed the human body to evolve in response to the soul's need for an adaptable body. Some people are horrified to consider that they may have descended from the apes, as it compromises their belief that God created humankind. This does not compromise that at all. What has been missing from the theory of evolution is why it took place. It took place for those reasons stated: the mutually adaptive process of the physical human form and the soul.

Early humankind was simple, primitive, apelike, but they were not apes. Souls do not have an evolutionary cycle within the animals of the lower-evolved brain species. The soul is very high level, and in order to function well and to achieve and create what is necessary for enlightenment it must exist within a physical container that will allow it to function to its fullest potential. On Earth, the human body is the only vehicle functioning at a level evolved enough to support a soul. The human body is unique and very purposeful in its existence. It did not randomly evolve and emerge; it was aided and directed by the highest form of energy available—the loving energy of God. The human form is not an accident, but was created by God as an act of love to provide a physical experience for his beloved children. You perceive your body as God's child, but remember it is your soul that is God's child. Your body becomes the child only as long as it houses the soul.

A body without a soul cannot exist. A physical body and a soul must join together in order for a body to be active and functioning. Most people are unaware of the wonderful abilities and characteristics of the physical body. My intent is to share some of this information, as it can assist as you consider your life journey from the soul perspective.

Your life on Earth is not a puzzle without all the pieces; you just have not always known where to find the missing pieces. Part of my purpose is to assist you in finding the pieces of information that will help you put together the puzzle that life can seem to be. As you put the pieces together, you will see your world more clearly. This view is from a new perspective, a soul perspective that is an empowering, wondrous view of all that is.

21

⊕

HEAVEN

I am often asked what it is like where I am. It is a most wondrous place in which to exist. It is a place of infinite joy, a place of unconditional love and acceptance. Heaven is a place which nurtures and honors the soul in its infinite oneness with God. But what is it really like, they ask? Are there houses or structures, do you eat, do you sleep, do you have friends, are there those who are in charge, do you have a boss, do you have a guide?

In the spirit world, we are pure energy in a place of pure energy. We are not far removed from your world, for we are layered together as one. Your world is one that vibrates at a slower rate than mine and that lower vibration creates a denser energy, which structures into matter, giving shape to your reality. That form is maintained by the belief or the thought that it exists. Because it is believed to exist, it does.

As a soul, I am pure energy. I have no form, therefore no need for a world of form through which to express. You, too, when you choose, will be a part of this formless world, and you will realize how we and the people of Earth coexist in the same place. We exist within varying degrees of expressed energy and this is all that separates us.

In the need to understand and to relate to the spirit world, information has often been presented in a way that is more readily understood by people. As a means to help people understand it, the spirit realm has often been presented as a place with structure. Heaven, or the spirit realm, has also been described as having levels that one moves through according to degrees of awareness. While I do not particularly follow this line of thought, I would not say it is incorrect.

There are in the spirit realm many areas of interest and concentration, and a soul entering into the spirit realm may choose a particular area within which to work and exist. In this manner we compartmentalize, or segment, in order to concentrate our energies in a unified and directed way with other souls with similar interests. This grouping, however, does not suggest a hierarchy denoting a level of attainment. Where we choose to be and to assist is only suggested by our own personal unique experiences. In this realm we are able to create a reality of shape and form, and it is most often done when we assist souls transitioning from physical reality through the death process. With the goal of comfort and security for arriving souls, we create, from the information of a just-completed life experience, that scene that would most provide a feeling of safety and security for that soul. If the earthly experience led to an expectation of a heaven of white-winged angels with St. Peter standing at the gate with previously departed loved ones, then that is what can be created.

I have friends in the physical world who have welcomed me, befriended me, and graciously shared with me. I use the name Gerod only in connection with this channel. However, if you were to inquire about me through another channeled source you would discover they would be able to track me in this world of spirit. In this realm there are other guides with whom I am closely aligned because our work is similar in nature and because we may be providing guidance to people who in the physical world are connected in some way.

When I work with people responding to their questions, I am also in close contact with their guide. In my service it is very important for me to avoid intrusion and to avoid any disruption of free will. I assure you that in all situations I work with great caution and respect and I welcome the advice and assistance of these personal guides. They are to be highly commended in their diligence to protect the integrity of your experience on Earth.

Not all beings in the spirit realm are guides; there are other capacities in this world of spirit in which a soul may choose to work. Those particular roles are not as obvious to you as a role such as mine, but nonetheless they all play very important parts in this universe.

22

⊕

PHYSICAL HEALING

Healing is an ancient craft that evolved with the desire of humankind to alleviate suffering, to enhance life experience, and to facilitate prolonging life. In the earliest days of the primitive world which came after the demise on Earth of those more advanced societies, there was a collective thought energy which permeated the consciousness of the primitive society and aided people in the intuitive unfolding of their skills. Inherently, the soul always knew of the properties of energy for healing, but the involvement of rituals and medicinal herbs and stones as an adjunct to that energy was inherited from the ancient civilizations.

That pool of collective thought became very instrumental in developing the aspect of healing as a facet of human existence. The experience of illness, disease, and disability, as well as the experience of healing, has been a profoundly important aspect of the experience available to souls in the physical. It is the avenue through which the limits of the physical body are explored in order to realize the illusionary quality of the body in comparison to the soul.

Humankind has moved from primitive medicine into medical practice so unlimited that it endlessly raises questions regarding the moral obligations. Basically, with the skills that have been developed, humans play God. I see the dilemma that this advancing knowledge creates; these are the situations that force humans to finally examine the issue of soul and the spiritual nature of humans. Questions, issues, and debate are important to humans, as they are the impetus to internal examination. Experiences lead to questions and contemplation which will produce expansion and growth; hence, the need for the medical and moral dilemma.

These types of medical and ethical questions will never have answers that will satisfy all, for every situation needs to be evaluated on its own merit. In this society, the consciousness of Earth has not yet evolved where it can allow for that type of nondiscriminatory justice. Time will bring you ever closer to that acceptance and realization, but until you reach that point these experiences are the forces to keep you moving there.

Energy is powerful when high level, clean and fluid—fluid in the sense that the energy is not hampered by the denser vibration of matter. Therefore, when you wish to utilize energy as a healing tool, you need to tap into fluid energy, which exists only outside of the world of matter. It can be channeled into your world and used to manifest and affect healing, but once it has done its work it is absorbed, and becomes nonfluid energy. That is why energy healings must be incorporated as a way of life to continuously enhance high-level soul energy within the body. Many people can offer their own energy as a form of healing. If their energy is high level, enhanced with love and light, they can indeed have some healing effect on the one with whom they work. However, as this is personal energy housed within a body and localized within matter, it is therefore limited in its ability to effect a high-level energy healing.

As people have become more open to ancient healing practices, high-level healing energy has been offered. Many energy techniques and practices have been on Earth for a long time; however, awareness was not always open to exploration of these healing energies. More recently, there has been a reintroduction of these techniques into the world, and they have been openly and lovingly received. Many people currently involved with these energies are those souls who have worked with them in previous incarnations. It is now time to reintroduce them back into the world. Not that many of these techniques ever left the world; they were just guarded carefully, as they were once more vulnerable.

There are many energies, and this does cause confusion. However, remember, as each soul is unique and different, each thought that created a particular healing energy is unique and individualized. Energy channeled into your reality for healing purposes has its creator and its continued source, and each is unique. In this dimension of spirit, there are many varied souls and responsibilities which have led to the varied forms of healing energies. I will not at this time explore and explain each of these energies, for they will come into your life should it be appropriate. However, suffice it to say that the energy techniques and healing processes you will hear of will be many. Some healing energies will be more effective for some people than for others, and while many people may channel the same energy, it will come through each person somewhat differently. Because energy comes through in a pure state, it is affected by the energy of the one who brings it in. Therefore, it is incumbent upon each person to be aware of with whom they work.

No harm can be generated by high-level energy directed for healing, but just because someone purports to have received a specific healing energy to use and share does not always mean that they use it with the utmost love and respect. The universe is careful of energy, but again, free will exists, and we will not interfere with choices made at the level of your reality. A person of low intentions can obtain a healing energy, for whatever reason, but the energy will not be as effective when channeled through a being of low-level dense energy. This, however, is not a blanket statement of the abilities and intentions of those who do not spectacularly channel the healing energy they have accessed. I am saying: be a human of intent and purpose and know with whom you work if you wish to access high-level healing energy.

As time moves on, you will see the face of medicine changing as it adds dimension and character to its functioning by accessing the spiritual dimension. Bodywork, energy work, and healing with all accessible avenues of information available will be the norm. People will have more choices available to them, and as people demand respect for their choices the medical community will take note. There will be new practices and standards adapted that will incorporate spiritual healing with current and future medical practices. This is the direction of the soul, and thus, this is the direction of your world.

23

$\oplus$

THE SHIFT

As you read these words, you participate in the distribution of high-level energy to your world. As you read, at your deepest level you hear my words.

Within you at a deep level is that high-level energy that is your soul. The information I share here is from the Light. Your soul, created in the Light, resonates with the energy of this information and draws to your consciousness awareness of your soul.

Through conscious awareness of the energy of the soul self, one is more readily able to accept high-level energy into the physical body, which in a sense, then, one shares with the physical world. This is how individuals assist in the expansion of knowledge and awareness in the physical world. This energy supports contemplative exploration of the spiritual principles.

When people raise their vibrational energy through expansion of conscious awareness they are contributing to the enhancement of the entire physical world and are assisting a global awareness that can transform the world. This transformation is a shift in consciousness, yet it is also an actual physical shift in the physical universe and it is one that has long been prophesized. Many have warned that it is a cataclysmic shift that will bring physical and emotional distress; some have even considered this shift will end the world.

Your planet is undergoing a physical shift. A very slight axis change, nearly unintelligible to current instruments of measurement, is occurring. The entire planet is shifting and minutely and discreetly repositioning itself within the galaxy.

In the spirit realm we are aware of this process. In order to assist the transition, to have it be comfortable, we provide information to enrich your knowledge, which also enhances the quality of energy on Earth.

All over your world people are breaking the chains of bondage and oppression, seeking the birthright of all, not given by humankind, but given by God: the freedom to be, to choose, and to express. As people strive for these human rights, they strive for their rights as beings of the universe, not just beings of this one world.

People knowingly long for what is denied to them through the corruption of human rights. The strength to fight for freedom, to insist on rights of choice, is a high-level energy that seeks expression through many means. While the expression is often violent, it is still part of the unfolding. When at last peace and freedom prevail, the world will still operate within the confines of physical laws, but the principles and truths will be those of the unlimited spirit. This is what will change the physical world from one of physically dense energy to one that hums and glows with the light of a more highly evolved vibrational energy.

With the shift in the Earth's vibratory rate not all people will be able to exist on Earth, as their souls will not be compatible with the enhanced vibration. As the energy of Earth and its collective consciousness becomes vibrationally finer, the experience of life on Earth will change; it will shift. With this shift some individuals will find that that their energy is no longer compatible with Earth, which will make it uncomfortable for them to continue their life experience on it. As the shift approaches, another planet will be made available for them for Earth will become a place of high-level energy, a world inhabited by high-level beings within a physical body. For those not yet ready to transcend to a higher vibration it does not mean their soul is inadequate or unable, it is only that a soul chooses experiences that correspond to its level of understanding of itself. It is important for you to have an understanding acceptance of your soul; where you are and what you do at this moment is exactly where you need to be.

This enhancement of Earth is a slow, gradual process, and the signs of its unfolding are global as well as personal. It is painful, as individually, people struggle on many levels. In the mass consciousness, society struggles as well.

Consider your desire to understand yourself and your existence. For reasons you may not fully comprehend you know you are more than blood and bone and tissue; you know you cannot be merely an accident or a curious evolution of nature. The feeling of knowingness within you refuses to disregard existence. You think, therefore, you are. You exist.

Through your questions, your curiosity, and your probing you and people like you will change. In your search for understanding you become aware and open and you allow your inner light, the vision of that light from which it came. The journey is yours, but on the way you enhance the world you live in.

Thank you for hearing me. God bless you.

24

⊕

EARTH SPIRITS

Earth spirits are souls from the spirit realm that enhance and amplify energy of particular events occurring in the physical world. I am not speaking of earthbound spirits; they are something quite different altogether. The Earth spirits of which I speak are high-level souls of light who carry into the physical reality not only their own light and energy, but also additional energy with which to infuse a particular unfolding when it may be helpful. This is not an intrusive action, because the energy they bring is positive high-level loving energy. It is brought in for those who may need it because of their participation in a particular event that needs the highest support possible. There are times when Earth spirits may bring energy in response to large-scale crises affecting large numbers of people, such as natural disasters like earthquakes, hurricanes, or tornadoes. It is also offered in times of civil strife when the actions of few devastatingly affect many such as in the attack on the World Trade Center building in New York City, or in other political or military conflicts where people are being killed.

These Earth spirits actually take human form when they come to Earth bringing this energy. The physical form is necessary in order to condense this high vibrational energy into a form that can be infused into the world of matter. Were it not stepped down in this way, this high-level energy would not be compatible enough to be utilized. The Earth spirits create a body and place themselves within a large group of people close to the unfolding situation. Should the critical point of infusion involve only a very small, select group of people where an unknown character would stand out, the Earth spirit will commune at the soul level with a soul already present in a physical body and attempt to obtain that soul's permission to enter and allow that high level energy to be diffused through that person's body. This does not disrupt or intrude, but merely offers the assistance of loving positive energy should it be the wish of a soul to utilize it.

There are other beings that are like Earth spirits. However, they come to Earth not in response to crisis situations, but to anchor the Light of God to

Earth in order to enhance the energy and unfolding of Earth. Like the Earth spirits, these beings create a body through which to diffuse high-level energy. I refer to these beings as points of light.

25

PROGRAMMERS, SEARCHERS, ELDERS AND PLANNERS

In the spirit realm between lives a soul is in a wondrous time of reflection: reflection upon the life it has just left, on its entire history, and on the possibilities for future experiences in the physical world.

As a soul seeking awareness through experience, it has a responsibility to look at what has occurred in the life experience and to look at what needs to be further explored and expanded. The result of this contemplative reflection, coupled with the assistance of advisors in the spirit realm, will lead each soul to important decisions about its next experience. For many, reflection will make obvious what work is still in progress and what needs further exploration. It may mean a need to live through a physical incarnation once again with particular souls. In that case, there is a large scale undertaking to orchestrate, since the time and place of a soul's reentry into the physical reality may need to coordinate with the presence of others.

High-level programmers assist with reentry into the physical. Those souls who do this work assist in choosing the time, place, and entry family, in order for a soul to have the maximum possibility for achieving what it is it wishes to achieve in that particular Earth experience. The programmers, gifted with vision that encompasses many levels of existence at once, are able to pinpoint the critical points of entry and those potential influences that enhance the experience. While all of us in spirit form are able to see the bigger picture of existence, we are not as focused as the programmers are. Programmers are specialized, working for the best probable life for each soul with whom they work. They are dedicated to this loving assistance.

All of us assist you in the physical world. You have not been cast adrift without assistance. As well as the programmer who assists you into your time and place in the physical reality, you have a personal guide. There are also others from the spirit world who assist you, both directly and indirectly. The titles

I assign to these various roles are my own. However, should you inquire, there are others who know these beings by these titles also.

There are those whom I call the searchers. The searchers are those who travel extensively, usually solitarily, to seek out unfolding events and people who may be in need of assistance. The searcher brings to the spirit world information about people, places, and unfolding events that may need particular assistance from the spirit world. The attention needed may be handled in a variety of ways. If a situation is unfolding that may have profound impact, there is a consultation with the elders. The elders review the situation to decide if the spirit world will become involved. If it is appropriate to offer divine energy into this situation in a greater way then that decision will be lovingly made by the council of elders. The elders are not beings superior to any other soul, but are merely those souls who have agreed to accept the responsibility of making those decisions. As with any being, because they work exclusively in a particular area, they become skilled in their work and thus their opinions and advice are highly regarded.

The spirit world treads very lightly in the world of humans. We will not upset the laws of your world that ensure physical existence, and we will not interfere with free will. However, there are times when the wisdom of the searcher recognizes a need for assistance. The wise searcher carries this information home to the council of elders for discussion and decision.

Once the council of elders decides assistance will be given, the planners determine how that will be accomplished. The responsibilities of the planners are voluminous, as they must review Earth history and the probable potentials of the future. They must also look into the souls of the key players; those individuals in the physical who are or will be needed to play a role in that particular unfolding event. As I describe this work of spirit you may have already realized that one example of a spirit-assisted unfolding is that of the historical existence of Jesus Christ upon your Earth.

Once the plan is developed, it is set in motion through the directed energies of all souls in the spirit realm. Once the plan goes into motion, it is energy—free to evolve into what it will. I assure you that all participants in the physical are well-guided, and they choose at the soul level to participate in the unfolding to fulfill not only the lessons of the world, but also the lessons of their own personal need. Again, this is affirmation that no event occurs for one single person or unfolding.

26

○

DIVINE ORDER

As you read the information I have presented, I wish to express my appreciation for your attention and thoughtfulness to it. Some who read this material may feel that there is a nonspecificity about the world of spirit and wonder how the world of spirit can have the ability to affect the universe if it does not have order to it.

I assure you, there is order to the universe. We are all created from one point of existence; therefore, it is only our perceived awareness of separation that actually separates us. When we relinquish the illusion of separateness, we will find ourselves in divine harmony with all that is. In this state of cohesive being, we are fully aware of the oneness that exists. We understand that divine order is recognizing and accepting all that is as a perfect state of oneness that does not require structure. Structure does not create divine order; love and recognition of our oneness is what creates divine order.

I am often asked to explain the hierarchy of heaven: what levels exist, what is required for a soul to move from one level to another. People wish to know what level I am from and what level they are from. They want to know about angels and archangels, saints and guides. They ask about divas, fairies, elementals, good spirits, and evil spirits.

People of Earth wish to attach a structure to the spirit realm to help them relate to it. In the world of matter, people understand structures: social structures, business structures, educational structures, family structures, and for the most part they understand the workings of those structures and their place within them. Through examination of one's formal education, financial attainment, community service, familial connections and social contacts, individuals superficially evaluate themselves and others.

Within the physical reality, these structures have validity as they facilitate human experience. However, if human experience is learning to process life with all aspects of the being, then it is necessary to employ the spiritual aspects of the self in that processing. As hearts expand in awareness of spiritual truths, it becomes obvious that evaluating a person by an external structure is an illusionary process. External evaluation of an individual is judging their actions in relationship to the physical reality and not becoming aware of the whole individual. The true value of accepting is loving compassion toward all individuals, whatever their status in the physical reality.

A person who is financially charitable is a generous person. However, perhaps the person is not so generous if the charitable act is not done out of love, but rather out of fear. One who is not financially charitable, yet is neither unkind nor cruel, and is loving and compassionate, can be very generous indeed. However, if the person does not act outwardly in a way visible within the structure, such as giving large sums of money to the poor, there may not be recognition of the loving charity of that person's heart.

What I am saying is this: be cautious, be wary, of evaluating the worth, the truth, the value of any person and any situation by the structure it appears to exist within.

If someone were to ask me specifics about the hierarchy of the spirit realm and levels a soul may encounter, I would tell them nothing, as this is not my way of teaching. Guides are highly individualized. Therefore, we have our areas of interest, our areas of expertise. My way of teaching is to avoid the use of a structure such as a hierarchy. I relate from the soul level and attempt to detach from structure as a form for discernment and evaluation. It is as if I were the artist who asks you to close your eyes and see not with your eyes, not with your mind, but with your heart.

My belief is that when you see, think, and feel from the energy of your heart, you enhance the vitality of your life force and move yourself into expanding awareness. Individuals in the physical body think, feel, and expand their awareness in different ways. Therefore, some people will not feel comfortable exploring universal existence within the confines of a structure, while others need more concrete structures within which to explore concepts. For that reason, spiritual frameworks do exist; they are governed by spirit guides who feel comfortable maintaining and teaching within that structure. In this way we are able to teach and offer spiritual information and experience in a way that has comfort and appeal to many people. Just as it takes many different kinds of books to get across the same idea, it can take many concepts of the spiritual universe to open humans to the consciousness of expanded awareness.

Understand this: there is no right way, no wrong way, in which to perceive the spiritual universe. If you need a structured spiritual hierarchy, a plan and process set forth to adhere to in your spiritual quest, then it is there for you. However, if you are one who cannot expand as freely within a hierarchal plan, then you are free to abandon the belief that such a structure is necessary.

One way is not superior to another. One way does not mean someone is more advanced than others. The only right way is the way that is appropriate for a particular individual at a particular time. To judge the rightness of one path over another would be in error. To allow each person their choice without gloating over your choice is generous love.

It is important to walk your path in love. I would not wish you to use the universe and any hierarchal structures as tools to prolong self-judgment and the judgment of others. God loves you as you are. Love others, also, as they are.

27

TRUTH SEEKERS

As humankind has evolved, the human mind has expanded. In that expansion has been the birth of creative thought that allows people to ponder and thoughtfully examine their existence. With self-examination comes the realization that humans are more than mere physical beings. In that realization is born the need to understand more.

Truth-seekers are spiritual people willing to explore and experiment to find the boundaries of their faith in order to expand them. They are in search of expanded understanding, and are open and willing to examine and explore alternatives and possibilities in order to gain knowledge and enhance awareness. Truth-seekers can be flamboyant in their quest or very quiet and private. They are willing to share their knowledge as they listen to others, and they take responsibility for their choices as they acknowledge the choices of others. Truth-seekers are willing to be tolerant, compassionate, and respectful of all persons, wherever they may be in their journey.

One does not have to be any religion to know God. No particular group, no one spiritual leader has the infinite truth. It belongs to all and is available to all who look within.

28

◎

THE TAPESTRY

The view of All That Is available in the spirit realm is highly evolved. It is a tapestry: large, beautiful, a work of art; it is not one-dimensional, it is multi-layered. As you examine its pattern, you may completely lose a particular thread at one point, only to discover it reemerging within a different scene at a different location in the tapestry. Looking closely at the other threads in the scene you will discover they were all together many times before in other scenes within this brilliant tapestry.

You will see that as the layers of threads merge and emerge to create a scene, they are laying the unseen groundwork for the next scene. You come to realize that a thread cannot exist alone. Were you to remove a thread it would become linear. Without shape or substance, it is no longer part of the experience of the tapestry. Each thread is a unique part of the whole. It enhances the presentation of particular scenes with its own unique color and texture; the scene would be incomplete without that particular thread

Created of light and energy, this is the tapestry of All That Is. It is complete and yet incomplete, for it is a tapestry started at the center that expands and grows. It lives and breathes. The tapestry is you and me and all the others. It is God's creation of love.

This tapestry is self-reliant. All that it is and all that it needs is within it and all that it must be it is. We here in the spirit world are able to see this tapestry of which we are a part, and of which you are a part, and we wish for you to use your inner vision to see it also. It will help you understand that humans on Earth are not separate from the spirit world, for we are threads intertwined and we all meet and merge in various places within that beautiful tapestry. We are all one, of that there is no doubt.

29

◎

CLOSING

As I conclude this book, I wish to share these thoughts. Have compassion not only for your companions, but also for yourself. You are alive within a human body because this is the experience you have chosen. Honor your choice and your experience by imbuing your actions with love and integrity. You need only acknowledge your oneness with the creator to acknowledge your oneness with all people and all that is.

Realize that each individual soul is on a very personal journey of transformation that is brought about as we recognize ourselves and accept ourselves as infinite beings of the universe. In the process of transformation, we come to realize the sacredness of each soul's journey, and we step aside and offer love and support to all we encounter. For those we do not understand, do not like, and do not trust, we can offer compassion.

Realize that love is the act of offering freedom to all souls to be what they are. Love is the act that brings hearts to the truth. Love is the force that holds the universe together. Love is all that is necessary.

Made in the USA
Middletown, DE
02 June 2017